the Silver Grille

Favorite Recipes from Higbee's Silver Grille

Judith Karberg
Jane Hazen

PUBLISHING INFORMATION

Published by
Cleveland Landmarks Press, Inc.
13610 Shaker Boulevard, Suite 503
Cleveland, Ohio 44120-1592
(216) 658 4144

www.clevelandlandmarkspress.com

Second Printing

ISBN 978-0-936760-35-3

Library of Congress Control Number
2013949928

Designed by
John Yasenosky, III

Printed by
Bookmasters
Ashland, Ohio

TABLE OF CONTENTS

PREFACE

It was in summer 1999 that Cleveland art professor and historian Richard Karberg approached Cleveland Landmarks Press. He had an idea for a book about Higbee's Silver Grille restaurant. He wanted to make memories of the then-shuttered restaurant once again come alive. And to make sure that happened as fully as possible, he decided to incorporate some favorite recipes from the Grille into his story.

Ready and willing, Karberg's wife Judith and her good friend Jane Hazen dove into the storehouse of Silver Grille recipes that had been preserved by former Higbee's employees. Those recipes, of course, had been detailed for large numbers of diners, and so Judith and Jane went to work reducing them to family-size portions and to tinkering with the list of ingredients to reflect the changes in culinary arts that the passage of decades had brought about.

The result of these efforts was the 2000 publication of *The Silver Grille: Memories and Recipes*. The book was a great success, and so it was followed in 2001 by *The Higbee Company and the Silver Grille: More Memories, More Recipes*.

Both books have been out of print since 2007, but callers have continued to ask Cleveland Landmarks Press about a possible reprint of the recipes. With the renewed interest in The Higbee Company that has been spurred by the opening of Horseshoe Casino in the Higbee Building, the timing seemed right to republish a volume of the Grille's recipes, combined from both previous books. The result is this *Favorite Recipes from Higbee's Silver Grille*, a volume of 117 popular Silver Grille recipes.

Good cooking!

ACKNOWLEDGMENTS

We acknowledge once again those individuals who provided Silver Grille information for our original exploration of the restaurant in *The Silver Grille: Memories and Recipes*: Ann Zupancic, Jim McDonnell, and Margaret Hetterline.

And since this book is about recipes, we gratefully acknowledge those who helped test the recipes appearing again in this book. These include: Jeanne Hudson, Jerry Maddox, Laurie Ross, Carla Keller, Carolyn Dessin, Flo Worth Spencer, Michael D. Powell, Gerry Burdick, Cathy Brown, Janice Bogges, Marilyn Wilson, and Mary Sopinski.

And finally, we again acknowledge the work of Judith Karberg and Jane Hazen for once again meticulously checking the ingredients and instructions for each recipe. Thanks also to Cleveland Landmark Press' partner, Gregory G. Deegan, for his proofreading and to John Yasenosky, III, for his fresh design of the final product.

The image on the back cover shows the renovated Silver Grille set up for an event *(Mark Weiland photo, courtesy Ritz Carlton Hotel)*. Other images are from the Richard Karberg Collection, unless otherwise noted.

James A. Toman
Publisher
July 2013

INTRODUCTION

Restaurants typically have an ephemeral existence. Changes in ownership or management frequently portend a predictable demise. Changing tastes often steer once loyal customers to the offerings of new venues. Such famous names in Cleveland dining as the Clark's and Stouffer's restaurant chains illustrate the reality.

Higbee's Silver Grille tea room on the store's 10th floor proved an exception to the rule. For 58 years the Grille catered to a loyal clientele. Over that lengthy time span, The Silver Grille served lunch six days each week (seven when the store adopted Sunday business hours) and for many years it also was host to high tea and even to dinner when the store stayed open late. Employees report that several hundred patrons were served every day, and that number would escalate to well over a thousand when the Grille provided food for special events in the Higbee Auditorium or Lounge. Taking these elements into consideration, it is a reasonable estimate to conclude that over the years The Silver Grille probably served approximately 10 million meals. Those meals not only provided delicious fare, they also created indelible memories.

Into the 1960s the menu in the Silver Grille was changed daily, although certain specialties and seasonal items remained on the menu for extended periods of time. The pleasure received by a diner at The Silver Grille was the result of many years of hard work in establishing the recipes.

The numerous volumes of the still extant Silver Grille recipe books and their accompanying cost guides provide a glimpse into what it was like to run such a restaurant. Pages in these volumes broke down the ingredients by amount and by the per-serving costs, and they recorded the changes in cost that took place over the years. Handwritten notes accompanying these guides provided the caveat that specific dishes were to be prepared only when their ingredients were not cost prohibitive. This statement had particular application to vegetables, and especially to tomatoes, in the years when locally grown produce was used. During a time when there were truly seasonal variations of ingredients, these comments had to be taken seriously. As transportation services advanced, many food ingredients became available year-round, and so some featured dishes on the menu became regular rather than seasonal

Instructions about ingredients also reveal that these recipes grew out of the era of the Great Depression. Muffin crumbs the next day became part of the toppings for the various crisps. Meat scraps were put to use as well. Few ready-prepared items were used, and rarer still were brand names of commercial food products. One exception was the use of Schrafft's Chocolate Liquor, which was not an alcoholic product, but instead a thinned syrup.

From time to time, Higbee's added new recipes to its menu. Ideas came from a variety of sources, including what was popular in the restaurants of other stores to which Higbee's was linked by its membership in the Associated Merchandise Corporation. New recipes also came from featured items in the food section of newspapers and magazines and from what appealed to a changing American sense of taste.

The selection of recipes in this volume provides a look at many favorites. Included are entrees, soups and salads, side dishes, breads and muffins, cakes, and pies.

Bon appétit!

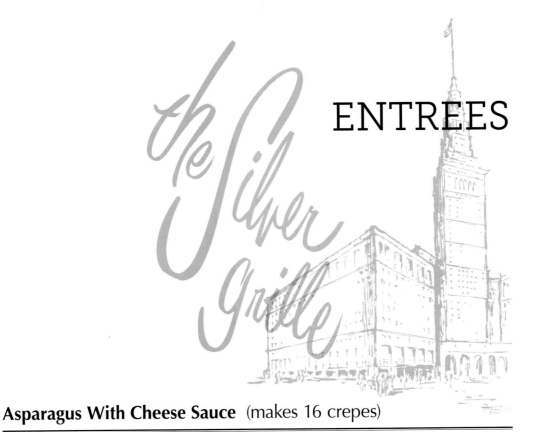

the Silver Grille

Asparagus With Cheese Sauce (makes 16 crepes)

1 cup	milk
¾ cup	chablis
½ cup	grated cheddar cheese
2 Tbsps.	flour
2 Tbsps.	butter
Pinch	salt

Melt butter, add flour and stir. Add milk, stirring constantly, and cook until thickened. Add cheese, stir to blend, and add Chablis and seasonings. Place 4 cooked asparagus spears in crepe, and roll. Pour 4½ Tbsps. cheese sauce over the filled crepe (see following recipe).

Garnish with 3 slices of lightly sauteed mushrooms

Crepe Batter:

4	whole eggs
4	egg yolks
1 cup	milk
¾ cup	flour
	Salt to taste

Mix flour, eggs, and egg yolks with a wire whisk. Add milk and salt, and beat until thoroughly blended. Heat a small skillet, and brush with oil. Put in enough batter (1-2 Tbsps.), and tilt pan immediately so that the batter will spread over the entire bottom of the pan. Cook the crepe quickly on both sides. Repeat the process until all the crepes are cooked, stacking them on a plate as they are finished; cover with a sheet of wax paper to prevent drying out.

Entrees

Baked Cheese Soufflé (serves 8)

3 cups	scalded milk
4 cups	fresh bread crumbs
10 ozs.	grated American cheese
1 Tbsp.	melted butter
4 large	well-beaten egg yolks
4 large	egg whites, beaten until stiff
1 tsp.	salt
¼ tsp.	pepper
⅓ tsp.	dry mustard

Place bread crumbs in a large bowl. Add grated cheese, melted butter, and seasonings. Pour scalded milk over the mixture, and stir to blend. Gradually fold in beaten egg yolks, then the beaten egg whites. Place in a well-buttered 9" by 13" casserole or 8 oz. custard cups. Bake in a 350-degree oven for 40 minutes until the top is golden brown. Best when served with a mushroom sauce.

Baked Chicken Breasts in Sour Cream (serves 4)

1 cup	sour cream
2 tsps.	soy sauce
½ tsp.	garlic salt
2 Tbsps.	lemon juice
1 tsp.	celery salt
1 tsp.	paprika
dash	pepper
2 cups	seasoned bread crumbs 4 chicken breasts, 6 ounces each
4 Tbsps.	melted butter

Mix together sour cream, soy sauce, garlic salt, lemon juice, celery salt, paprika, and pepper.

Dip chicken into mixture, and then roll in the seasoned bread crumbs. Arrange pieces in a lightly greased baking dish. Drizzle with the melted butter, and bake uncovered in a 350-degree oven for 45-60 minutes.

Entrees

Baked Chicken Loaf (serves 4-6)

½ cup	coarsely chopped chicken
⅔ cup	soft bread crumbs
⅓ cup	cooked rice
1½ Tbsps.	butter
⅓ cup	chicken broth
2 Tbsps.	chopped pimentos
⅓ tsp.	salt
⅓ tsp.	paprika
2	well-beaten eggs

Mix the ingredients in the order given above. Put into greased loaf pan 4" by 8" by 4" lined with wax paper. Bake in a moderate oven (325 to 350 degrees) one hour or until loaf is set.

Note: This recipe was served cold, with french fries and a fruit salad.
It can also be served warm with the chicken cream sauce

Baked Ham Loaf (serves 4)

¾ lb.	ground ham
½ lb.	ground pork
½ lb.	ground veal
1	egg
⅓ cup	bread crumbs
⅓ cup	cream sauce (see recipe below)

Combine all of the ingredients, and mix well. Place in a greased meat loaf pan.
Top with a mixture of:

½ tsp.	ground cloves.
½ tsp.	dry mustard
2⅔ Tbsps.	sugar

Bake in a 375-degree oven for 45 – 60 minutes. Serve with mustard sauce: combine 1 cup mayonnaise and 2 Tbsp. prepared mustard.

Cream Sauce for Ham Loaf

2 Tbsps.	butter or margarine
2 Tbsps.	flour
1 cup	hot milk
¼ tsp.	salt
⅛ tsp.	pepper
1 drop	yellow food coloring

Melt the butter or margarine in a saucepan over low heat. Blend in the flour, and cook approximately 3 minutes or until bubbly. Slowly add the hot milk, stirring constantly. Bring to a full boil, and add seasonings and food coloring.

Baked Macaroni and Cheese (serves 4)

½ lb.	raw macaroni, cooked according to directions
½ lb.	grated cheddar or American cheese
½ cup	butter or margarine
½ cup	flour
1½ tsps.	salt
⅛ tsp.	pepper
4 cups	hot milk

Melt butter or margarine until hot, and add flour, stirring constantly until it comes to a foam.

Add hot milk in small amounts, stirring constantly. Add seasonings. When mixture comes to a full boil, remove it from the stove, and add the cheese. Stir until the cheese melts, and then fold in the cooked macaroni. Mix well, and place in a buttered casserole. Bake in a 350-degree oven for 30 minutes.

Bavarian Pork and Sauerkraut (serves 6)

¼ cup	butter or margarine
1¼ lbs.	pork cubes
½ Tbsp.	onion, chopped
¾ tsp.	paprika
¾ tsp.	salt
¼ tsp.	pepper
4 cups	drained sauerkraut
2 Tbsps.	brown sugar
¼ cup	sour cream

Brown meat in butter or margarine. Add onion, paprika, salt, and pepper. Cook until meat is tender. If it gets dry, add a little chicken broth or water. Add brown sugar and sauerkraut. Cook about 1 hour longer. Just before serving, add the sour cream and mix well.

Note: The tester suggests increasing onion to ½ cup, chopped; this entree tastes better the next day.

Beef Strogonoff (makes 10 cups)

2½ lbs.	beef strips
½ cup	margarine
1 large	onion, sliced
4 cups	hot beef broth
	salt, pepper, garlic powder to taste
1 lb.	sliced mushrooms
¾ cup	flour
1 cup	water
½ cup	red wine
1 cup	sour cream

Cut meat into ½" by 1½" strips. Brown meat in margarine. Add onions. Cook about 1 hour or until meat is tender. Add hot broth, seasonings, and wine. Bring to a boil. Add mushrooms, and cook until the mushrooms are done. Combine flour and water (strain so there are no lumps), and add to the meat mixture. Bring to a full boil, and cook about 5 minutes. Remove from heat, and blend in the sour cream.

Chicken Pot Pie (makes 4 servings)

5 cups	cream sauce (see recipe below)
3 cups	diced or pulled chicken meat
¾ cup	fresh or frozen peas
1 cup	fresh or frozen carrots
	pie crust dough or puff pastry

Combine all ingredients into individual or family style baking dish(es) and cover with your favorite pie crust or puff pastry top. Bake until crust is browned (per your crust directions).

Cream Sauce for Chicken Pot Pie (makes 4 cups)

⅓ cup	butter
½ cup + 2 Tbsps.	flour
4 cups	water
2 Tbsps.	chicken base
⅓ Tbsp.	yellow food coloring
	Salt to taste

Combine melted butter and flour over a low heat until it bubbles. Slowly add the water, constantly stirring until the mixture is smooth. Add the remainder of the ingredients, and whip until smooth.

Note: Tester chose not to use yellow food coloring.

Higbee's Championship Chili (serves 6-8)

2 lbs.	coarse ground sirloin
1	finely chopped onion
1 clove	(minced) garlic
8 oz. can	of tomato sauce
1 can	condensed tomato soup
1 cup	water
3 Tbsps.	chili powder
¼ tsp.	cayenne pepper
1 Tbsp.	salt
1 Tbsp.	paprika
½ tsp.	ground pepper
¼ tsp.	ground cumin
¼ cup	flour mixed with ½ cup water

Sauté meat in large sauce pan. Add onions and garlic; cook until onion is soft. Stir in remaining ingredients except flour and water. Cover and simmer for 1 hour. Remove lid, and allow to simmer until excess moisture evaporates (do not let it get too dry). Add flour mixture, and cook until thickened (about 5-10 minutes). Stir, and do not allow mix to get too dry.

Higbee's Special Sandwich

1 square	dark rye bread
1 oz.	turkey breast slice
1 oz.	Swiss cheese slice
1 oz.	Canadian bacon slice
1 cup	Thousand Island dressing
	Iceberg lettuce
1 slice	tomato
1 slice	hard-boiled egg
1	pitted black olive
1 slice	cooked bacon

Butter the bread on one side, and place buttered side up on a serving dish. Place on the bread the turkey slice, a small leaf of lettuce, the cheese, another leaf of lettuce, and then the Canadian bacon, all in a stack. Cover with a large outer leaf of lettuce, making a dome over the sandwich. Pour the dressing over the dome. On a toothpick, spear the tomato, egg, and black olive, and use to garnish the very top of the dome. Serve with the bacon slice on the side.

Entrees

Hungarian Stuffed Cabbage Rolls (makes 20 cabbage rolls)

1 lb.	ground pork
1 lb.	ground beef
2 cups	cooked rice
1 tsp.	salt
dash	pepper
¼ cup	milk
1	egg
¼ cup	chopped onion
1½ heads	cabbage
2 cups	stewed tomatoes

Combine the ingredients (except the cabbage and tomatoes) and mix well. Use a number 20 scoop (¼ cup) to place mixture on softened cabbage leaves. Place the meatballs on partially cooked cabbage leaves. Roll them up and place in a baking dish. Cover with stewed tomatoes (or 2 cups of cut-up canned tomatoes). Bake in a 400-degree oven for 1 hour. Make the tomato sauce (see recipe below), and pour over the cabbage rolls. Cover with a lid or foil and bake 1 hour longer.

Tomato Sauce for Cabbage Rolls

2 Tbsps.	margarine or butter
5 Tbsps.	chopped onion
4 Tbsps.	flour
2 cups	canned tomatoes
	Paprika, salt, and pepper to taste
1½ cups	cream sauce (see recipe below)
2 qts.	shredded cabbage
1 cup	sour cream

Sauté onions in margarine or butter. Add flour and cook about 5 minutes. Add stewed tomatoes and seasonings. Add cream sauce and shredded cabbage. Cook until cabbage is almost done. Remove from stove and add sour cream; mix well. Pour the sauce over the cabbage rolls. Cover and bake in a 400-degree oven for 1 hour.

Cream Sauce for Cabbage Rolls (makes about 6 servings)

1½ Tbsps.	butter or margarine
1½ Tbsps.	flour
1½ cups	hot milk

Heat butter or margarine, blend in flour, and cook until foamy. Add hot milk, stirring constantly, and bring to a full boil.

Hungarian Veal Balls

1½ lbs.	ground veal
dash	garlic powder
2½ Tbsps.	chopped parsley
1 tsp.	salt
dash	pepper
5 Tbsps.	milk
2	eggs
10 Tbsps.	bread crumbs

Combine all ingredients and mix well. Shape meat into size of small walnuts (about 32 balls) and place into baking pan. Bake in 325-degree oven for about 30 minutes. Drain off liquid. Make sauce recipe (see below) and pour over the balls. Then bake 30 minutes longer. Serve with buttered egg noodles or small dumplings.

Sour Cream Sauce for Veal Balls

6 Tbsps.	margarine
1 Tbsp.	chopped onion
⅛ tsp.	paprika
¼ cup	flour
1½ cups	chicken broth, heated
½ cup	sour cream
	Salt to taste
	Pepper to taste

Sauté onions in margarine with paprika until they are tender. Add flour and cook about 3 minutes. Add hot chicken broth and bring to a boil. Taste for seasonings and add salt and pepper as desired. Remove from heat, add sour cream and pour over the veal balls.

Hint: If desired, make twice the amount of sauce so there is plenty for the noodles or dumplings.

Macaroni and Cheese Soufflé (serves 4-6)

1 cup	fresh bread crumbs
1⅓ cup	scalded milk
½ lb.	grated American cheese
3	egg yolks beaten
¼ cup	chopped pimento
2 Tbsps.	melted butter
1 Tbsp.	chopped parsley
1 Tbsp.	chopped onion
¼ tsp.	salt
3	egg whites beaten stiff
¼ tsp.	cream of tartar
1⅓ cups	cooked macaroni

Combine soft bread crumbs, grated cheese, butter, and salt. Add scalded milk, and mix. Blend in beaten egg yolks until lemon-colored. Add pimento, parsley, onions, and cooked macaroni. Fold in beaten egg whites to which cream of tartar has been added. Place in a buttered casserole dish. Place casserole in a pan of hot water and bake in a 350-degree oven for 1 hour or until firm.

Quiche Lorraine (makes 1 quiche)

1	partially baked pie crust shell (baked 5 minutes in 450-degree oven)
¾ cup	bacon bits
1 cup	shredded Swiss cheese
4	eggs
1 tsp.	chopped onion
2 cups	half and half
½ tsp.	salt
¼ tsp.	sugar
⅛ tsp.	black pepper

Sprinkle bacon, cheese and, onion into baked pie shell. Beat eggs lightly, and then beat in remaining ingredients. Pour cream mixture into the pie shell. Bake pie in a 350-degree oven for 30 minutes or until knife inserted comes out clean.

Note: Tester used an unbaked pie shell and increased baking time slightly. A variation would omit bacon bits, onion, and sugar, and instead substitute ½ tsp. nutmeg and 10 oz. cooked spinach–squeezed in a towel to remove excess water–and baked as above.

Seafood Pie (serves 6)

⅓ cup	butter or margarine
⅓ cup	flour
½ tsp.	salt
2 cups	liquid from fish liquor and milk, fish stock, or
	diluted cream of mushroom soup
2 Tbsps.	chopped onion
1 cup	frozen carrots, peas, or celery (or a combination of these)
1 can (16 ozs.)	flaked and drained salmon
	Pastry for a 1 crust pie

Melt butter in a large saucepan or skillet. Stir in flour and salt, and blend until smooth. Add liquid gradually, and cook until thickened, stirring constantly. Add onion, vegetables and salmon. Blend thoroughly. Pour into a well-greased 8- or 9-inch pie plate or 1½ -quart casserole dish. Top with the pastry which has been marked with several slits. Bake at 425 degrees about 30 minutes or until crust is lightly browned and casserole is heated through.

Note: If desired, 2 to 3 cups of halibut, cooked and flaked, may be substituted for the salmon.

Shrimp Newburg (serves 6)

1¼ lbs.	medium shrimp, cooked
6 cups	hot cream sauce (see recipe below)
3 Tbsps.	butter
3 Tbsps.	chopped onion
1 tsp.	lemon juice
1 tsp.	paprika
½ tsp.	salt
dash	pepper
dash	cayenne pepper
4 Tbsps.	white wine or sherry

Sauté onions in butter until transparent; then add paprika, shrimp, and lemon juice. Add cream sauce, seasonings, and wine.

Cream Sauce for Shrimp Newburg

¾ cup	butter or margarine
¾ cup	flour
6 cups	hot milk
1½ tsps.	salt
1 tsp.	pepper
3 or 4 drops	egg color (optional)

Melt butter in a sauce pan over low heat, whisk in the flour. Cook about 3 minutes or until bubbly. Slowly add the hot milk, stirring constantly. Bring to a full boil, and add seasonings and color.

Spaghetti Bake With Tomato and Cheese (makes 6 cups)

4 ozs.	spaghetti
4 Tbsps.	margarine
1¼ cups	chopped onion
1 cup	chopped green pepper
2½ cups	diced tomatoes
1 tsp.	salt
4 oz.	grated American cheese
⅛ tsp.	black pepper

Cook spaghetti in boiling water until tender. Drain. Sauté onions, green pepper, and tomatoes until vegetables are tender, about 30 minutes. Add the cooked spaghetti, cheese, and seasonings, and mix well. Place in a 350-degree oven about 30 minutes or until bubbly. If mixture seems dry, add a little water.

Note: Tester says that while this is not "traditional" spaghetti, it makes a very tasty pasta dish.

Tuna A La King (serves 6)

½ cup	margarine
½ cup	flour
4 cups	hot milk
¾ tsp.	salt
⅛ tsp.	pepper
¼ cup	diced pimento
½ cup	cooked green pepper strips
½ cup	mushrooms sauteed in 2 to 3 tsp. margarine
2 6-oz. cans	tuna fish, drained and flaked

Heat margarine, add flour, and cook about 3 minutes. Add hot milk, stirring constantly, and bring to a boil. Add the seasonings. Blend in the rest of the ingredients. Serve with rice, noodles, or pastry biscuit.

Welsh Rarebit (makes 5 cups)

8 Tbsps.	butter or margarine
1 tsp.	paprika
9 Tbsps.	flour
4 cups	hot milk
10 ozs.	grated sharp cheddar cheese, grated
1½ tsps.	Worcestershire sauce
¾ tsp.	salt
⅛ tsp.	white pepper

Melt butter or margarine until hot, and then add the flour, stirring constantly about 5 minutes or until the mixture bubbles. Pour in the hot milk in small amounts, stirring constantly until the sauce is smooth. Add the Worcestershire sauce and seasonings. Remove from the stove, and stir in the grated cheese, mixing until cheese is melted. Keep hot. Garnish each serving with 7 whole almonds.

Note: In the 1933 version, beef fat was used in this recipe.
The rarebit was served over triangles of thinly sliced, toasted white bread.

Soups and Side Dishes

Au Gratin Potatoes (makes 7 cups)

5 cups	cooked and diced potatoes
6 Tbsps.	margarine
6 Tbsps.	flour
3 cups	hot milk
1 tsp.	salt
$\frac{1}{8}$ tsp.	pepper
$\frac{3}{4}$ lb.	grated cheddar cheese

Melt margarine until hot; then add flour, stirring constantly about 3 minutes. Add milk in small amounts at a time, stirring constantly. Add seasonings, and bring to a full boil. Remove from heat, add the grated cheese, and blend thoroughly. Gently fold in the cooked potatoes. Mix well.

Pour into a 4-quart greased casserole. Bake in a 325-degree oven about 45 minutes or until bubbly. During the last 5 minutes you may add more cheese on top.

Canadian Cheese Soup (makes 8 cups)

1 qt.	chicken broth
$\frac{1}{2}$ cup	diced carrots
$\frac{1}{4}$ cup	diced celery
1 qt.	milk
$\frac{1}{4}$ cup	butter
$\frac{1}{2}$ cup	chopped onion
$\frac{1}{4}$ cup	flour
$4\frac{1}{2}$ tsps.	cornstarch

Pinch	baking soda
¼ tsp.	paprika
Pinch	salt
1 cup	grated cheddar cheese
1 Tbsp.	chopped parsley

Sauté onions in butter; then add flour, cornstarch, soda, paprika, and salt. Blend, and cook well. Add hot milk. Cook celery and carrots in stock. When tender, add to cream sauce. Add chopped parsley and cheddar cheese.

Cape Cod Chowder (makes 7 cups)

2 cups	diced potatoes
2 Tbsps.	margarine
1 cup	chopped onion
2 8-oz.	bottles of clam juice
2 6- or 8-oz.	cans of chopped clams
2 cups	hot milk
½ tsp.	crushed thyme
	Salt and pepper to taste

Peel and dice potatoes. Place in a 3 qt.-sauce pot, and cover with water until potatoes are tender. Drain. Meanwhile sauté the onions in the margarine until soft. Add the clam juice and milk, and bring to a boil. Add the potatoes and clams. Bring to a boil, and add the seasonings.

Corn Oysters (serves 4)

2 cups	corn, scraped from the cob (or frozen corn, thawed)
2	well beaten eggs
¼ cup	flour
¼ tsp.	baking powder
	Salt and pepper to taste

Mix together all ingredients and drop by teaspoon onto hot and greased griddle. Turn once when brown, brown second side, and serve.

Cream of Fresh Pea Soup (serves 6)

⅓ cup	margarine
3 Tbsps.	finely chopped onion
½ cup	flour
2⅓ cups	hot chicken broth
2 cups	hot milk

Soups and Side Dishes

²⁄₃ cup   hot half and half
2 cups   finely chopped cooked peas
          Salt and pepper to taste

Sauté onions in margarine until soft. Add flour and cook until foamy, about 5 minutes. Add hot chicken broth, milk, and cream in small amounts at a time, and bring to a full boil. Add the chopped peas and seasonings to taste.

Deviled Cheese Ball

     1 lb.   grated Cheddar cheese
2 Tbsps.   ketchup
    1 tsp.   Worcestershire sauce
  ½ tsp.   paprika
2 Tbsps.   margarine
  ½ tsp.   salt
  3 ozs.   chopped nuts

Combine ingredients (except for the chopped nuts) in an electric mixer in the order given. Beat until smooth and fluffy. Chill. Then form into a ball and roll it in the chopped nuts.

Russian Borscht Soup (makes 4½ cups)

  ¼ cup   butter or margarine
  ¼ cup   chopped onion
  ¼ cup   flour
 1 1-lb.   can of beets (reserve the juice)
Beet juice   (add enough water to make 1 cup)
  1 can   hot chicken broth
  1 cup   hot half and half
  1 tsp.   salt
  Pinch   pepper
  Pinch   ground cloves
  1 tsp.   white vinegar
          Sour cream for garnish

Sauté onions in butter until tender, add the flour, and cook about 3 minutes. Add the hot broth, juice, and cream, stirring constantly until it comes to a full boil. Add the seasonings and vinegar, and mix well. Add the grated beets. Garnish with sour cream.

Scalloped Tomatoes (serves 6)

1	chopped onion
4 Tbsps.	butter or margarine
2 slices	bread, cubed
¼ cup	brown sugar
4 cups	fresh tomatoes, cut up
½ tsp.	salt
¼ tsp.	pepper

Sauté onion in butter, add bread crumbs and brown sugar. Stir over low heat 3 to 5 minutes. Stir in tomatoes, and add seasonings. Pour mixture into greased 1-½ quart casserole. Bake in a 350-degree oven 30 minutes.

Swiss Rice (makes about 4 cups)

½ cup	finely chopped onion
¼ cup	finely chopped green pepper
3 Tbsps.	butter or margarine
1	1-lb. can of tomatoes
1 tsp.	salt
⅛ tsp.	pepper
3 cups	cooked rice
4 ozs. (1 cup)	shredded Swiss cheese

In a large skillet sauté and stir onions and green pepper in butter until the onions are tender. Stir in tomatoes, salt, pepper, and cooked rice. Simmer uncovered over low heat about 15 minutes until flavors are blended and the mixture is hot. Stir in Swiss cheese until well blended. Serve hot.

Yellow Custard Rice

2 cups	cooked rice
2	eggs
2 cups	milk
¼ tsp.	salt
⅛ tsp.	pepper
¾ tsp.	butter
1-2 drops	yellow food coloring

Combine all ingredients while rice is still hot. Mix well, and place in a buttered casserole which is placed in a pan of hot water. Bake in a 350-degree oven for 2 hours or until a knife inserted in the rice comes out clean.

Soups and Side Dishes

Salads and Dressings

Beef, Tomato, and Green Bean Salad (makes 4 small servings)

2 cups	shredded iceberg lettuce
1 cup	julienne cut roast beef
2 cups	celery, sliced
½ tsp.	onion, finely chopped
2 cups	green beans
1 cup	fresh tomato, diced

Cook fresh or frozen green beans until tender. Cool to room temperature. Marinate the roast beef in French dressing for 1 hour in the refrigerator. Add to other ingredients and serve immediately.

Cabbage, Carrot and Apple Salad

2 cups	cabbage, shredded
2 cups	carrots, shredded
1⅓ cups	apples, diced small
¼ cup	French dressing
½ Tbsp.	sugar
Dash	salt
Pinch	pepper

Combine cabbage, carrots and apples in a bowl. Pour dressing over all. Add salt and pepper, and toss well.

Glace Dressing for Fresh Fruit (makes about 1 cup)

6 tsps.	super fine sugar
1 tsp.	dry mustard
¼ tsp.	salt
3 Tbsps.	cider vinegar
7½ ozs.	salad oil
1½ tsps.	paprika
⅛ tsp.	onion juice

Combine all dry ingredients, and add vinegar and onion juice. Beat with an electric mixer until sugar is dissolved. Add oil in small amounts at a time, beating until thick – the consistency of mayonnaise.

Higbee's French Dressing (makes 1½ cups)

¾ cup	salad oil
2 Tbsps.	olive oil
6 Tbsps.	cider vinegar
2 Tbsps.	water
2 tsps.	sugar
1 tsp.	salt
½ tsp.	pepper

In a jar combine dry ingredients, and add vinegar and water. Shake to dissolve sugar, and add the oil and olive oil.   Shake.

Italian Dressing

½ cup	wine vinegar
½ cup	olive oil
1 cup	salad oil
½ clove	garlic, crushed
¼ tsp.	salt
¼ tsp.	oregano
¼ tsp.	celery salt
¼ tsp.	sugar

Mix all the ingredients. Store in refrigerator. Shake before using.

Marinated Fresh Vegetable Salad

½ cup   lima beans
½ cup   carrots
½ cup   peas
½ cup   celery
½ cup   green beans
1 cup   fresh tomatoes, diced
½ tsp.   salt
¼ tsp.   pepper
1 Tbsp.   onion, chopped fine
2 cups   iceberg lettuce finely shredded
2 cups   cabbage, finely shredded
¼ cup   French dressing

Use either fresh or frozen lima beans, peas, carrots, and green beans. If fresh, cook until just tender. If frozen, heat until just tender. Cool cooked vegetables to room temperature. Add to all the other ingredients and chill.

Maurice Salad (1 serving)

1½ cups   diced iceberg lettuce
1 oz.   julienned cooked ham
1 oz.   julienned cooked turkey or chicken
1 oz.   julienned Swiss cheese
1 tsp.   chopped sweet pickle

Combine all ingredients. Mix with ¼ cup of classic Maurice dressing and place in a bowl lined with lettuce leaves.

Classic Maurice Dressing (serves 4)
1 cup   mayonnaise
1   hard-boiled egg, chopped
2 Tbsps.   chopped parsley
1 tsp.   vinegar

Combine and mix.

Note: The original Maurice Dressing was made with a commercial base not currently available. This recipe was developed by a former Silver Grille employee.

Salads and Dressings

Potato and Egg Salad (makes 5 cups)

4 cups	cooked and diced potatoes
1 cup	sliced celery
¼ cup	oil and vinegar dressing
½ tsp.	chopped onion
1 cup	mayonnaise
1 tsp.	salt
Dash	pepper
2	hard-cooked and diced eggs

Dice potatoes while still hot, and marinate in oil and vinegar dressing. Add onions. When cool, add mayonnaise, celery, salt, and pepper, and gently mix in eggs. Refrigerate until serving time.

Russian Dressing (makes about 1 cup)

½ cup	mayonnaise
6 Tbsps.	chili sauce
2 Tbsps.	vinegar
1 Tbsp.	Worcestershire sauce
½ tsp.	salt
¼ cup	chopped pimento
¾ tsp.	grated onion
Pinch	pepper

Combine all the ingredients, and mix well. Store refrigerated in a covered jar.

Spinach and Apple Salad (makes 9 cups)

4 cups	washed spinach, cut into small pieces
1 cup	Delicious apples, diced
1 cup	peeled and seeded cucumbers, diced
1 tsp.	grated onion
¼ cup	Higbee French dressing, to which is added
4 tsps.	vinegar
1 Tbsp.	sugar
1 tsp.	salt
Pinch	pepper

Trim and wash spinach, and cut into small pieces. Dice apples into small cubes. Peel and seed cucumbers, and dice into small cubes. In a jar combine the rest of the ingredients, add to the spinach mixture, and toss well.

Salads and Dressings

Sweet and Sour Dressing

¼ cup	vinegar
2½ Tbsps.	sugar
¼ tsp.	oregano
¼ tsp.	basil
¾ tsp.	dry mustard
Pinch	salt
Dash	garlic powder
1 cup	salad oil
¼ cup	vinegar

Combine in mixing bowl first vinegar with sugar, oregano, basil, dry mustard, salt, and garlic powder. Mix well with an electric mixer. Beat in oil very gradually and continue until thick. Pour in the second vinegar and mix until blended.

Tomato Blossom With Diced Chicken Salad (serves 8)

1½ lbs.	cooked chicken, diced into large cubes
2 cups	chopped celery
1½ Tbsps.	fresh dill weed
½ cup	sour cream
1½ cup	mayonnaise
1 tsp.	salt
½ tsp.	pepper
1 per serving:	3 oz. tomato, bibb lettuce, and diced lettuce
8 slices	cucumber per serving
1	sliced hard-boiled egg per serving
1	ripe olive per serving
1	dill weed sprig per serving

Combine first 7 ingredients to make the chicken salad. Then, for each serving, line an 8" by 1" glass plate with bibb lettuce, and top with chopped lettuce. Place the tomato which has been star cut in the center of the bed of lettuce. Using a scoop, place ⅛ of the chicken salad in the center of the tomato. Fan out the sliced cucumbers on the left side of the plate. On the right side fan out the sliced egg. Sprinkle paprika over both. Garnish with an olive and dill weed.

Tuna and Sea Shell Salad (makes 3¾ cups)

4 ozs.	uncooked sea shell macaroni
2 6-oz. cans	tuna fish, drained and flaked
¼ cup	chopped celery
¼ cup	chopped green pepper
¼ cup	chopped pimento
1 tsp.	grated onion
1½ tsps.	vinegar
6 Tbsps.	mayonnaise
¾ tsp.	salt
Pinch	pepper

Cook sea shells according to package directions; then drain, rinse, and cool. Combine the rest of the ingredients, and toss well.

Vinaigrette Dressing

1½ cup	olive oil
½ cup	white wine
1 tsp.	minced garlic
1 cup	diced green onion
¼ cup	minced parsley
2 tsps.	dried oregano
2 tsps.	dried basil
1 tsp.	sea salt
¼ tsp.	ground pepper

Combine ingredients in a screw-top jar and refrigerate. Dressing congeals when refrigerated; bring to room temperature before serving.

Salads and Dressings

Breads and Muffins

Banana Bread (makes 4 loaves)

1 cup	margarine
4 cups	sugar
8	eggs
4 tsps.	baking soda
½ cup	water
6 cups	flour
3 cups	mashed bananas

Cream shortening and sugar together. Add eggs, and mix well. Dissolve the baking soda in water. Add the flour alternately with the baking soda. Mix well. Add the mashed bananas on slow speed of an electric mixer, mixing well. Divide into well-greased and floured loaf pans. Bake in a 350-degree oven for 1 hour.

Blueberry Muffins (makes 2 dozen)

½ cup	butter
2 Tbsps.	solid vegetable shortening
¾ cup	sugar
2	egg yolks
3½ cups	flour
3 Tbsps.	baking powder
1½ cups	fresh blueberries
2 cups	milk
2	egg whites
1 tsp.	salt

Cream butter and shortening. Add the sugar and then the egg yolks. Mix the flour and baking powder; add the blueberries. Stir until coated. Mix into creamed mixture with a spoon, alternating with the milk. Beat the egg whites and the salt until stiff. Fold gently into the first mixture. Bake in muffin pans lined with paper muffin cups for about 25 minutes at 350 degrees.

Cranberry Orange Bread (makes 3 loaves)

½ cup	margarine
1½ cups	sugar
1 cup	brown sugar
2 Tbsps.	grated orange rind
4	eggs
1 cup	orange juice
½ cup	milk
1 cup	chopped nuts
2 cups	whole or chopped cranberries (if using frozen berries, leave whole)
4 cups	flour
5 tsps.	baking powder
1½ tsp.	salt

Cream margarine, and add granulated sugar and brown sugar; cream well. Add orange rind and eggs; beat well. Combine orange juice and milk mixture. In another bowl combine the nuts, cranberries, flour, baking powder, and salt. Combine all ingredients and mix until moistened. Pour into 3 greased loaf pans lined with wax paper. Bake in a 350-degree oven for 1 hour. Cool in pans 5 to 10 minutes and then remove.

Topping:

	Juice of 2 oranges
1½ cups	sugar

Combine the orange juice and sugar, bring to a boil, and pour on the bread.

Herbed Biscuits

3 cups	flour
2 tsps.	salt
4 tsps.	baking powder
1 tsp.	baking soda
½ cup	shortening
4 Tbsps.	fresh minced chives
4 Tbsps.	fresh minced parsley
2	eggs
1½ cups	buttermilk
	Egg glaze (1 egg beaten with 1 tsp. water and a pinch of salt)

Place the flour, salt, baking powder, and baking soda in a mixing bowl, and cut in the shortening using 2 knives or a pastry blender. Continue rapidly until fat is broken up into pieces the size of coarse salt. Stir the herbs into the flour mixture. Blend the eggs in a large measuring cup, beat in the buttermilk, and mix rapidly into the flour with a rubber spatula, turning and pressing the ingredients together to form a dough. Scoop the dough out onto a lightly floured work surface, and with the floured heels of your hands rapidly knead the dough to give it enough body so it can be patted or rolled out (the less you work it, the more tender it will be, but it must have enough body to hold its shape softly). Place the dough on a lightly floured work surface. Pat it or roll it rapidly to a thickness of about ½″ and into the size of casserole dishes. Place over filled casserole, pressing dough lightly against the sides of casserole. Paint dough with a coating of egg glaze. Bake in a 400-degree oven about 20 minutes.

Higbee's Cinnamon Muffins (makes 2 dozen)

¾ cup	shortening
1 cup	sugar
3	egg yolks
4 cups	flour
2 Tbsps.	baking powder
1 tsp.	salt
2 cups	milk
2	egg whites, beaten

Topping:

½ tsp.	cinnamon
3 Tbsps.	sugar

Cream shortening; add sugar and egg yolks; cream well. Combine flour, salt, baking powder, and cinnamon. Add shortening mixture alternately with milk, only to moisten the batter. Gently fold in the beaten egg whites. Divide the batter into well-greased muffin tins. Sprinkle cinnamon sugar on top of the batter, and bake at 400 degrees for 20 minutes.

Breads and Muffins

Higbee's Fruit Muffins (makes 2 dozen muffins)

¾ cup	shortening
1 cup	sugar
3	egg yolks
4 cups	flour
1 tsp.	salt
2 Tbsps.	baking powder
2 cups	milk
3	egg whites, beaten
1 cup	chopped fruit, drained

Cream shortening; add sugar and egg yolks; cream well. Combine flour, salt, and baking powder, and add to shortening mixture, alternating with milk, only to moisten the batter. Add the fruit, and gently fold in the beaten egg whites. Divide the batter into well-greased muffin tins, and bake in a 400-degree oven for 20 minutes.

Higbee's Muffins (Classic) (makes 2 dozen muffins)

10 Tbsps.	shortening
1 cup	sugar
2	egg yolks
4 cups	flour
1 tsp.	salt
2 Tbsps.	baking powder
2 cups	milk
2	egg whites, beaten stiff

Cream shortening; add sugar and egg yolks; cream well. Combine flour, salt, and baking powder, and add to shortening mixture, alternating mixture with milk, enough only to moisten the batter. Add the beaten egg whites, gently folding them into the mix. Divide the batter into well-greased muffin tins, and bake in 400-degree oven for 20 minutes.

Breads and Muffins

Higbee's Muffins (Variation) (makes 2 dozen)

¾ cup	shortening
1 cup	sugar
3	egg yolks
1 tsp.	salt
2 Tbsps.	baking powder
2 cups	milk
3	egg whites, beaten
4 cups	flour

Cream shortening; add sugar and egg yolks, and cream well. Combine flour, salt, and baking powder, and add to shortening mixture, alternating mixture with milk only to moisten the batter. Add the beaten egg whites, gently folding them into the mix. Divide the batter into well-greased muffin tins, and bake in a 400-degree oven for 20 minutes.

Note: This is a variation on the classic Higbee's Muffin, calling for an extra egg and an additional 2 tablespoons of shortening. We suspect it was introduced, later in more prosperous times when ingredients were more readily available and a slightly richer muffin was desired.

Honey Corn Muffins (makes 1 dozen)

1¾ cups	flour
1¼ tsps.	baking powder
½ tsp.	salt
⅓ cup	cornmeal
4 Tbsps.	shortening
½ cup	diced apples
1	egg
1⅓ cups	milk
¼ cup	honey

Sift flour once and measure. Add baking powder and salt. Sift again. Add cornmeal. Combine egg, milk, honey, and shortening, and add all at once to the flour-cornmeal mixture, stirring only enough to dampen the flour. Fold in apples. Bake in well-greased muffin tin at 400 degrees for 20 minutes or until brown.

Breads and Muffins

Lemon Nut Bread (makes 2 loaves)

½ cup	butter
1½ cups	sugar
4	eggs
4 tsps.	lemon rind
4 cups	flour
5 tsps.	baking powder
1½ tsps.	salt
1½ cups	milk
1 cup	chopped nuts
4 Tbsps.	sugar
4 tsps.	lemon juice

Cream butter with sugar. Add eggs and lemon rind, and beat well. Combine flour, baking powder and salt, and add to sugar mixture alternately with milk. Fold in nuts, and pour into greased loaf pan lined with waxed paper. Bake at 350 degrees for 1 hour. Let cool 10 minutes. Remove from pan. Combine lemon juice and second sugar. Boil and pour over bread.

Orange Bread (makes 2 small loaves)

1½ cups	flour
2 tsps.	baking powder
2 Tbsps.	grated orange rind
⅓ tsp.	salt
½ cup + 1 Tbsp.	sugar
½ cup	milk
1	egg
2½ Tbsps.	cream

In a large bowl combine flour, baking powder, salt, and sugar. Sift ingredients, and add the orange rind. In another bowl beat the egg lightly with a whisk. Add the milk and cream. Add this mixture to the flour mixture. Fold in gently. Divide into 2 greased loaf pans. Bake in a 325-degree oven for 1 hour.

Breads and Muffins

Pumpkin Fruit Bread (makes 2 loaves)

2 cups	canned pumpkin
2 cups	sugar
⅔ cup	softened margarine
½ cup	water
3	eggs
2½ cups	flour
2 tsps.	baking soda
1 tsp.	salt
1 tsp.	cinnamon
½ tsp.	ground cloves
⅔ cup	chopped dates or raisins
⅔ cup	chopped nuts

Blend the first five ingredients, and beat for 1 minute. Then add the dry ingredients, and stir in the raisins and nuts. Pour into two greased loaf pans. Bake in a 325-degree oven for 50-60 minutes. Cool in pan for 5 minutes; then remove from pan and allow to cool completely.

Raisin Scones (makes 12 scones)

4 cups	flour
5 tsps.	baking powder
2 tsps.	salt
1 cup	shortening
6 Tbsps.	sugar

Combine ingredients, and blend well. Add to the mixture and stir until just moistened:

1 cup	milk
2	eggs
1 cup	raisins

Roll dough ½" thick, and cut into triangles or drop by spoon onto greased baking sheet. Brush with milk, and sprinkle with sugar. Bake in a 450-degree oven for 10-12 minutes.

Spicy Apple Bread (makes 2 loaves)

¾ cup	margarine
1½ cups	brown sugar
3	eggs
3 Tbsps.	vinegar combined with water to make 1 cup
1 tsp.	vanilla
3 cups	flour
1½ tsps.	baking soda
1 tsp.	salt
1½ tsps.	cinnamon
¾ tsp.	nutmeg
½ tsp.	allspice
¼ tsp.	cloves
2 cups	chopped apples
1 cup	chopped nuts

Cream margarine and sugar. Add eggs, and beat well. Add vinegar-water mixture and vanilla. Beat well. Add dry ingredients, and mix thoroughly. Stir in apples and nuts. Grease 2 loaf pans and line with wax paper. Divide the batter evenly between the pans. Bake in a 350-degree oven for 45 to 55 minutes.

Whole Wheat Muffins (makes 1 dozen)

1	egg
¾ cup	milk
½ cup	vegetable oil
1 cup	whole wheat flour
1 cup	white flour
⅓ cup	brown sugar
3 tsps.	baking powder
1 tsp.	salt

Preheat oven to 400 degrees. Grease muffin tins. Beat egg in medium bowl, and then stir in milk and oil. Stir in remaining ingredients at once, and mix until just moistened. Batter will be lumpy. Divide batter into the muffin tins, and bake about 20 minutes. Remove immediately from pan.

Breads and Muffins

Desserts

Almond Cream Pudding (serves 6)

4 Tbsps.	farina
6 Tbsps.	sugar
2 cups	hot milk
1	egg, separated with egg yolk beaten
¼ tsp.	vanilla extract
¼ tsp.	almond extract
Pinch	salt

Mix sugar and farina together. Add a small amount of the hot milk to dissolve the mixture, and then fold in the beaten egg yolk and flavorings. Cool until the pan is warm to the touch; fold in the beaten egg white. Pour into one serving dish or into individual dishes. Refrigerate.

Apple Brown Betty

5 cups	sliced apples
¾ cup	sugar
½ tsp.	cinnamon
¾ tsp.	lemon juice

Mix apples, sugar, cinnamon, and lemon juice, and place in greased baking pan.

Topping:

4 cups	Higbee's Muffin crumbs
¼ cup	butter
¼ cup	brown sugar

Mix ingredients together and spread over the top of the apple mixture. Bake in a 350-degree oven for 45 – 60 minutes.

Bread Pudding (serves 6)

3 cups	milk
4 Tbsps.	margarine
2	eggs
½ cup	sugar
¼ tsp.	salt
1 tsp.	cinnamon
3 cups	soft bread cubes
½ cup	raisins

Heat oven to 350 degrees. Scald milk, and add margarine. Beat eggs slightly in bowl; then stir in milk mixture, sugar, and cinnamon. Put bread cubes and raisins in a 1½ qt. buttered baking dish. Pour milk mixture over the bread cubes, and stir gently. Place dish in a pan of hot water. Bake 40 to 45 minutes or until a thin-bladed knife inserted 1 inch from the center comes out clean. Serve warm or cold with cream or whipped cream.

Butterscotch Brownies

½ cup	butter
1¼ cups	dark brown sugar
2	eggs
1 cup	flour
½ tsp.	salt
1 tsp.	baking powder
2 tsps.	vanilla
½ cup	chopped pecans

Melt the butter, and pour over the brown sugar. Add eggs, mixing with a spoon just until blended. Add vanilla, the dry ingredients, and then the pecans, mixing just until blended. Pour into a greased eight-inch square pan. Bake at 350 degrees about 25 minutes. Cool in pan, and cut into squares.

Caramel Pudding (serves 6)

3 Tbsps.	butter
4 Tbsps.	flour
1½ cups	brown sugar
1 cup	water
1 cup	milk
¼ tsp.	salt
3	egg yolks
¼ tsp.	salt

Melt butter in a saucepan. Add the flour, stirring constantly, to make a roux. Heat the milk, water, and salt together, and slowly add to the roux. Stir constantly until thickened. Add the brown sugar, cooking until dissolved. Mix the yolks in a small bowl, and add to them a small amount of the heated mixture. Then add back to the mix in saucepan, stirring constantly until bubbles appear and the mixture is thick. Put in small custard cups, and chill.

Fruit Squares (makes 16 2″ by 2″ servings)

½ cup	butter
½ cup	sugar
1 cup	cake flour
1	egg
¼ cup	diced walnuts
1 20-oz. can	cherry filling
	Powdered sugar

Grease and flour one 8″ by 8″ by 2″ pan. Cream butter, sugar, and eggs. Add flour; then stir in nuts. Spread ¾ of the dough in the pan, pressing down bottom and up sides, and then spread filling over dough. Put the remaining dough in dollops on top of pie filling. Bake in 350-degree oven 45 minutes.   Sprinkle powdered sugar on top while still warm.

Hot Pecan Sauce for Praline Ice Cream (makes 2 cups)

½ cup	margarine
1 cup	firmly packed brown sugar
½ cup	granulated sugar
¼ cup	milk
½ cup	toasted pecan pieces

In a saucepan melt margarine, and stir in brown sugar, granulated sugar, and milk; stir constantly over medium heat until sugar is dissolved. Stir in pecans.

Indian Pudding (serves 6)

2½ cups	milk
½ tsp.	salt
4 cups	cornmeal
¼ cup	molasses
½ tsp.	salt
½ tsp.	ginger
½ Tbsp.	butter

Combine the ingredients, and cook over low heat for 30 to 40 minutes, stirring often until very thick. Pour into serving dish(es). Cool. Serve with whipped cream.

Note: The original recipe from 1937 indicates that the Indian Pudding was served both in The Silver Grille and in the dining rooms in the Guildhall Building, which were also operated by the Silver Grille staff.

Maple Pecan Bavarian (serves 10)

¼ cup	cold water
1 Tbsp.	gelatin
1 cup	hot maple syrup
2	egg yolks
1½ cups	heavy cream, whipped
6 Tbsps.	chopped pecans

Dissolve gelatin in cold water, and add to the hot syrup. Beat egg yolks into the mixture, and mix well. When the mixture begins to set, fold in the beaten whipped cream and finally fold in the chopped nuts. Divide into 10 dessert dishes.

Molasses Crinkle Cookies (makes 2½ dozen)

¾ cup	margarine
1 cup	brown sugar
1	egg
¼ cup	molasses
2¼ cups	flour
2 tsps.	baking soda
¼ tsp.	salt
½ tsp.	cloves
1 tsp.	cinnamon
½ Tbsp.	ginger

Mix all wet ingredients well, add the dry ingredients, and stir well. Scoop into balls, roll in sugar, and place on cookie sheet. Bake in 375-degree oven 10 minutes.

Desserts

Old Fashioned Raisin Bars (makes 4 dozen bars)

1 cup	strong coffee
1 cup	raisins
1 cup	sugar
½ cup	salad oil
1	beaten egg
1¾ cups	flour
1 tsp.	baking soda
½ tsp.	cinnamon
½ tsp.	nutmeg
¼ tsp.	salt
¼ tsp.	allspice
⅛ tsp.	cloves

Pour hot coffee over the raisins. Cool to lukewarm. Stir in sugar, oil, and egg. Stir together flour, soda, cinnamon, nutmeg, salt, allspice, and cloves; add raisin mixture and stir until combined. Pour into a greased 9" by 13" pan. Bake in a 375-degree oven for 12 to 15 minutes or until done. Cool. Spread with coffee icing, and sprinkle with ½ cup of nuts if desired.

Orange Tea Donuts

3½ cups	flour
3 Tbsps.	baking powder
1 tsp.	salt
7 Tbsps.	butter
7 ozs.	milk

Sift together flour, baking powder, and salt. Cut in butter, as for pie crust. Add milk all at once, mixing until flour is moistened. Flour hands, shape dough, and spread out to be cut with a 2-inch biscuit cutter. Place on greased pan, and bake 15 minutes in a 425-degree oven.

Note: This recipe, when tested, turned out to be neither donuts nor orange flavored. It is, however, the best biscuit recipe the tester has ever used.

Pineapple Nut Cookies (makes about 60 cookies)

1 cup	butter or margarine
1 cup	sugar
2	eggs
4½ cups	flour
½ tsp.	salt
2 tsps.	baking powder
½ tsp.	baking soda dissolved in 1 tsp. hot water
2 tsps.	vanilla
1½ Tbsps.	pineapple juice
1 cup	crushed pineapple (well drained)
1 cup	chopped pecans or walnuts

Drain the canned pineapple well, reserving 1½ Tbsp. of juice. Cream butter, and add sugar; then add slightly beaten eggs. Add dry ingredients alternately with pineapple juice and pineapple. Gently mix in nuts. Mixture will be stiff. Roll dough into golf ball size pieces, and place a few inches apart on a greased cookie sheet. Press down balls with the bottom of a glass dipped in sugar. Bake at 350 degrees 10 – 12 minutes, until bottoms are lightly browned.

Rice Bavarian Cream (serves 6)

1¾ tsps.	gelatin
⅛ cup	cold water
⅜ cup	cooked rice
⅛ cup	boiling water
Dash	salt
1 cup	whipping cream
6 Tbsps.	confectioners sugar
¼ tsp.	vanilla

Soak gelatin in cold water. Then add boiling water to dissolve gelatin. Add well-cooked rice and sugar (they should be so well cooked that the mixture is quite mushy). When this mixture is cool, fold in the cream, which has been whipped, and the vanilla. Put the mixture into individual serving dishes and chill.

Sand Bars

½ cup   butter
1⅓ cups flour
⅓ cup   finely chopped pecans
½ cup   sugar
1 tsp.   vanilla

Cream butter and sugar. Add flour, pecans, and vanilla. Press into bottom of lightly greased eight-inch square pan. Bake at 350 degrees about 20 to 30 minutes until lightly browned. Cool on rack until slightly warm, and cut with a thin sharp knife into bars.

Note: These will remind you of a popular "sandie" cookie!

Scotch Shortbread

2 cups   flour
2 tsps.   baking powder
¼ tsp.   salt
1 cup   butter
½ cup   confectioner's sugar

Sift the first three ingredients together and set aside. Make sure the butter is at room temperature. Cream the butter until fluffy, and add the sugar slowly, beating until light. Stir in the dry ingredients. Mixture will be very stiff and may require mixing by hand. Divide the dough in half and press each half into the bottom of a 9-inch glass pie plate. Score the dough into 8 wedges with a sharp knife. You may decorate the shortbread with the tines of a fork or a small cookie stamp before baking. Then bake at 350 degrees for 20 to 25 minutes, watching carefully. Bake until the edges are just browning. Remove from the oven, and cut through immediately in the score marks. Let cool completely in pan, and then remove carefully (shortbreads are fragile).

the Silver Grille

SOUPS AND APPETIZERS

Cream of Celery Soup	15-25
Chicken Consomme	15-25
Iced Tomato Juice	15-25
Iced Orange Juice	20-30

Salad Specialties

Yellow Cling Peach with Creamed Cottage
Cheese and Glace Dressing 75
A Tossed Green Salad with Julienne Ham
and Swiss Cheese with French or
Russian Dressing 95
Tunafish Salad with Sliced Tomatoes ... 1.25
A Higbee Mixed Salad 95
(Lettuce, Avocado Pear, Celery, Sliced Egg
and Anchovy, Roquefort Cheese Dressing)
Sliced Chicken with Fresh Fruit Sections . 1.50
A Fresh Fruit Salad Bowl, Glace Dressing
or Pineapple French Dressing 85
Hot Muffins or Hard Roll
Served with Above Salad

Sandwiches

Corned Beef Sandwich on Rye Bread with
Mustard and Dill Pickle 85
Bacon, Lettuce and Tomato 75
Sliced Breast of Chicken on White Bread .. 95
Higbee Special Sandwich 90
(Swiss Cheese, Canadian Bacon, White
Meat of Turkey, Russian Dressing and
Garnish of Tomato and Sliced Egg)
Minced Chicken Salad Sandwich 65
Tunafish Salad Sandwich 65
Chopped Egg and Watercress on
on Whole Wheat Bread 50
Baked Ham on Rye Bread 65
Toasted Cheese Sandwich 60
Served on Toast 5¢ Extra

DESSERTS, CHILLED SWEETS

Butterscotch Cream Pie, Whipped Cream . 25
Apple Pie 25
Hot Mince Pie 25
Angel Food Cake with Strawberries and
Whipped Cream 25
Cherry Cobbler with Whipped Cream 25
Imperial Cheddar Cheese with
Toasted Crackers 25
Apricot Halves 25
Fruit Jello with Whipped Cream 25
Red Raspberry, Pineapple or Orange
Sherbet 20
Peppermint Stick, Mint, Chocolate, Vanilla
or Coffee Ice Cream 20
Marshmallow, Butterscotch, Chocolate
or Pineapple Sundae 25
Cup of Diced Fresh Fruits 25

BEVERAGES

Metrecal with a Pot of Coffee 75
Chocolate Milk Shake 35
Chocolate Malted Milk 40
Pot of Tea, Orange Pekoe or Green Tea .. 15

Desserts

Cakes and Frostings

Angel Food Cake

1 cup	flour
1²/₃ cups	egg whites
½ tsp.	salt
1⅛ tsps.	cream of tartar
1½ cups	sugar
1 tsp.	vanilla

Sift flour 3 or 4 times. Beat egg whites until frothy. Sprinkle salt and cream of tartar over top, and continue beating until egg whites are just stiff enough to form peaks, but not dry. (If egg whites are thick and not watery, 2 Tbsps. of water may be sprinkled over the egg whites while adding cream of tartar and salt). Gradually fold in the sugar, sprinkling about 2 Tbsps. at a time over the surface. Fold in the flavoring. Gradually fold in the flour, sifting about ¼ cup at a time over the surface. Turn batter into an ungreased tube pan, and bake in a moderately slow oven, 325 degrees about 1 hour. Invert pan until cake is cold and then remove from pan. Serve with Strawberry Whipped Cream (see below).

Strawberry Whipped Cream
1 cup	whipping cream
¼ tsp.	lemon juice
2 Tbsps.	frozen strawberries, thawed

Whip cream and fold in strawberries and lemon juice.

Applesauce Cake (eight-inch layer cake)

½ cup	butter
2 cups	sugar
2	eggs
2½ cups	flour
¼ tsps.	baking powder
1½ tsps.	baking soda
1½ tsps.	salt
¾ tsp.	cinnamon
½ tsp.	ground cloves
¼ tsp.	allspice
½ cup	cold water
1½ cups	applesauce

Cream butter, add sugar and then eggs. Add sifted dry ingredients alternately with the cold water. Add in applesauce and mix gently. Bake in two well-greased and floured 8-inch layer cake pans at 375 degrees for 30 to 40 minutes. Cool for five minutes in pans; then remove, and cool on racks. Frost with butter cream frosting.

Butter Cream Frosting (for an eight-inch two-layer cake)

½ cup	butter
4 Tbsps.	solid vegetable shortening
3 cups	powdered sugar
2 Tbsps.	cream (approximate)

Beat butter and shortening until creamy. Gradually add the powdered sugar, adding in the cream as you go to thin slightly. Beat on high until thick and creamy.

Cheddar Chip Cheesecake

Crust:

1⅓ cups	graham cracker crumbs
5 Tbsps.	plus 1 tsp. melted butter
5 Tbsps.	plus 1 tsp. sugar
1 tsp.	ground cinnamon
5 Tbsps.	plus 1 tsp. ground nuts

Combine all ingredients; mix well. Pat into a buttered 9-inch spring-form pan. Press firmly onto bottom and 1 inch up the sides of the pan. Chill.

Cakes and Frostings

Filling:

1 lb.	cream cheese at room temperature
1½ Tbsps.	flour
⅔ cup	eggs, slightly beaten
1½ Tbsps.	milk
2 cups	cheddar cheese, shredded
1½ tsps.	vanilla extract
¾ cup	sugar

Soften cream cheese at room temperature. Whip at high speed of mixer for 3 minutes. Decrease speed to medium, and beat in half of the eggs. Beat at high speed 1 minute. Add cheddar cheese, sugar, and flour. Beat at low speed until well mixed. At medium speed beat in the milk, vanilla, and the remaining eggs. Beat at high speed one minute. Pour filling into chilled crust. Bake at 350 degrees 30-45 minutes or until set and a knife blade inserted into the cake comes out clean.

Note: This is a lighter version of the cheesecake we have become accustomed to. The cream cheese gives it some of the familiar tang while the cheddar cheese imparts a quiet but warm richness.

Chocolate Icing

4 Tbsps.	margarine or butter
3 cups	powdered sugar
⅓ cup	chocolate morsels, melted
3-4 Tbsps.	hot water

Cream butter, and then add partly cooled chocolate. Mix in powdered sugar, thinning with hot water as needed. Beat on high until thick and creamy.

Coffee Icing

3 Tbsps.	margarine
2 cups	powdered sugar
1 tsp.	vanilla
	Strong coffee

Cream margarine and sugar together; then add vanilla and enough coffee for spreading consistency.

Cakes and Frostings

Fruited Marshmallow Frosting (frosting for 1 two-layer cake)

1 cup	sugar
¼ cup	water
2	egg whites
¼ tsp.	cream of tartar
¼ tsp.	vanilla
6 Tbsps.	chopped dates
4 Tbsps.	chopped candied cherries
4 Tbsps.	raisins

Make a syrup of water and sugar. When the syrup reaches 215 degrees on a candy thermometer, start beating the egg whites in a separate bowl, adding the cream of tartar. When the syrup reaches 225 degrees, remove from heat, and in a fine drizzle, add to the beaten egg whites, and continue to beat for approximately 10 minutes, or until heavy and shiny. Add the vanilla. Fold in the dates, cherries, and raisins. Frost the bottom layer, assemble the cake, and frost the top and sides.

Fudge Upside Down Cake (serves 8)

Sift together:

1 cup	flour
¼ tsp.	salt
¾ cup	sugar
2 tsps.	baking powder

Add:

½ cup	milk
2 Tbsps.	melted butter
1 oz.	melted chocolate
1 tsp.	vanilla
½ cup	chopped nuts

Mix together all of the above and pour into a buttered 8″ by 8″ by 2″ pan.
Top with a mixture of:

½ cup	granulated sugar
3 Tbsps.	cocoa
½ cup	brown sugar
	Place 1 cup hot water over it all.

Bake 40 minutes in a 325-degree oven.

Indian Coconut Rice Cake

1½ cups butter
1 cup sugar
4 egg yolks
¾ cup farina
½ cup sifted flour
1 tsp. baking powder
1½ cups chopped coconut
1 tsp. vanilla
4 beaten egg whites

Cream butter, add sugar, and beat until light and fluffy. Add egg yolks. Sift farina, flour, and baking powder together; then add to butter mixture, and beat again. Add coconut and vanilla, and mix well. Beat egg whites until stiff but not dry, and fold into the mixture. Divide batter into 2 buttered and floured cake pans. Bake in preheated 350-degree oven 20 to 24 minutes. Cool on rack; then frost with fruited marshmallow frosting.

Lemon Chiffon Cake

2¼ cups flour
1½ cups sugar
1 Tbsp. baking powder
1 tsp. salt
½ cup salad oil
6 eggs, separated
2 Tbsps. lemon juice
1 tsp. grated lemon rind
1 tsp. cream of tartar
¾ cup cold water

Mix all dry ingredients in a large bowl. Add in order the oil, egg yolks, water, lemon juice, and rind, and beat until smooth. Beat the egg whites and the cream of tartar until very stiff. Pour the first mixture over the egg whites, carefully folding it in with a rubber scraper just until blended. Do not stir. Pour immediately into an ungreased angel-food cake pan (a tube pan with straight sides). Bake at 325 degrees for about 70 minutes. Cool upside down in pan supported in the center.

Cakes and Frostings

Light Fruit Cake

½ cup	butter
1¼ cups	brown sugar
2	egg yolks
⅔ cup	milk
2¼ cups	flour
3½ tsps.	baking powder
1 tsp.	almond extract
1 tsp.	vanilla
2 tsps.	coffee extract (optional)
½ cup	raisins
⅓ cup	currants
½ cup	walnuts
2 Tbsps.	grated orange rind
2	egg whites

Beat butter, and add the brown sugar, then the egg yolks. Blend the dry ingredients, and add alternately with the milk. Add the extracts, then the raisins, currants, walnuts, and orange rind. Beat the egg whites until stiff, and fold into the first mixture. Pour into a well-greased and floured loaf pan. Bake at 350 degrees for 50 to 60 minutes, or until the top springs back to the touch. Remove from pan after about five minutes, and cool on rack.

Maple Syrup Layer Cake

½ cup	butter
¼ cup	sugar
2	eggs
1 cup	maple syrup
2½ cups	flour
⅔ Tbsp.	baking powder
¾ tsp.	baking soda
½ tsp.	salt
1 cup	hot water

Beat the butter until creamy; add the sugar, then the eggs. Mix in the maple syrup. Mix the dry ingredients, and add alternately with the hot water. Butter and flour two eight-inch cake pans. Bake for 20 to 30 minutes at 350 degrees. Let cool in pans 5 – 10 minutes; then remove and cool on racks. Frost with maple syrup frosting.

Cakes and Frostings

Maple Syrup Frosting

     1 cup   brown sugar
    ¼ cup.   maple syrup
    ¼ tsp.   cream of tartar
      2   large egg whites (or equivalent amount of meringue powder)

Beat the egg whites with the cream of tartar until stiff. Gradually add in the sugar and maple syrup. It will frost an eight-inch two-layer cake.

Note: This recipe is presented as originally written. However, with new food safety guidelines, it is wise to use either pasteurized eggs or meringue powder, available in most major groceries.

Mexican Chocolate Cake

    2 cups   sifted flour
    2 cups   sugar
     1 tsp.   baking soda
     1 tsp.   salt
     1 tsp.   ground cinnamon
    ½ tsp.   baking powder
    ¾ cup   water
    ¾ cup   buttermilk
    ½ cup   shortening
      2   eggs
    4 ozs.   melted unsweetened chocolate
     1 tsp.   vanilla

Sift together flour, sugar, baking soda, salt, cinnamon, and baking powder into a large mixing bowl. Add water, buttermilk, shortening, eggs, melted chocolate, and vanilla. Blend 30 seconds in a mixer at low speed, scraping sides and bottom of the bowl occasionally. Spread batter evenly in a greased and floured 13″ by 9″ by 2″ pan or two 9″ round layer cake pans. Bake in a 350-degree oven 40 to 50 minutes (for large pan) or 30 to 35 minutes (for layer pans). Cool pans on a rack. Spread cooled cake with chocolate frosting.

Cakes and Frostings

Mexican Chocolate Frosting

½ cup   butter or margarine
2 ozs.   unsweetened chocolate.
¼ cup   milk
1 lb.   sifted powdered sugar
1 tsp.   vanilla
½ cup   chopped walnuts

Combine butter, chocolate, and milk in saucepan; heat until bubbles form around the edge of the pan, stirring occasionally. Remove from heat, and add the sifted powdered sugar, vanilla, and chopped nuts. Beat until spreading consistency. If necessary, add 1 to 2 Tbsps. of milk. Spread on cooled chocolate cake.

Orange Butter

1 lb.   margarine
Grated rind of one orange
2 Tbsps.   orange juice
1 oz.   orange flavored liquor

Bring margarine to room temperature, and whip in mixer. Grate oranges adding the grated skin to the margarine. Add the juice of the orange (1 oz.). Add orange flavored liquor to taste. Whip until volume doubles, and store in a sealed container under refrigeration.

Note: This is especially good on the lemon nut bread

Pineapple Upside Down Cake

½ cup   butter
1 cup + 2 Tbsps.   sugar
2   eggs
2 cups   flour
3 tsps.   baking powder
1 tsp.   salt
¾ cup   milk
1 tsp.   vanilla
1 cup   brown sugar
1 20-oz.   can of crushed pineapple, drained

Cream butter. Mix all the dry ingredients, and add to butter. Add half the milk and the vanilla. Beat for 2 minutes. Add the eggs and the rest of the milk. Beat for two minutes, scraping down sides and bottom of mixing bowl. Grease an eight-inch square pan. Pack onto the bottom 1 cup brown sugar. Drain well the 20-ounce can of crushed pineapple. Pour the drained pineapple over the brown sugar. Pour the cake batter over all. Bake at 350 degrees for 40 to 45 minutes. Cool, and serve right from the pan.

Pound Cake (makes one small loaf)

¾ stick	butter
1 cup	powdered sugar
1⅓ cups	flour
2	eggs
½ tsp.	rum flavoring or 1 tsp. vanilla
½ tsp.	mace
1 tsp.	lemon juice
⅓ cup. + 1 Tbsp.	milk

Beat butter until smooth. Add powdered sugar, and beat until well incorporated. Add the eggs, and beat until thick and lemon colored, about three or four minutes. Mix in flavorings; then add flour alternately with the milk. Beat well about another two minutes. Pour into a well-greased and floured loaf pan. Bake at 350 degrees for about 45 minutes. Turn out on rack to cool.

Red Velvet Cake (eight-inch two-layer cake)

½ cup	butter or margarine
1½ cups	sugar
2	eggs
2½ cups	flour
2 Tbsps.	cocoa
Pinch	salt
1 tsp.	baking soda
1 tsp.	vinegar
1 tsp.	vanilla
1 cup	buttermilk
8-10 drops	red food coloring

Beat butter until creamy, and add sugar. Mix in eggs. Add the dry ingredients alternately with the buttermilk and vinegar. Mix in vanilla and food coloring. Pour into two eight-inch round pans that have been greased and floured. Bake at 350 degrees for about 20 to 25 minutes. Cool about five minutes in pan; then finish cooling on racks. Frost with chocolate icing.

Cakes and Frostings

Toasted Coconut Upside Down Cake

7 Tbsps.	butter
2 cups	cake flour
1⅜ cup	sugar
3⅓ tsp.	baking powder
1 tsp.	salt
⅚ cup	milk
1 tsp.	vanilla
2	eggs

Cream butter on medium speed in mixer for one minute. Sift flour, sugar, baking powder, and salt. Add flour mixture, stirring to blend. Add one half the milk and the vanilla. Beat 2 minutes on low speed in a mixer. Add the eggs and remaining milk. Beat 1 minute in a mixer at medium speed. Scrape down the bowl, and beat 1 minute more. Bake in a greased and floured pan (9 x 13 inch) in a 350-degree oven 25 – 35 minutes.

Topping:

7 Tbsps.	butter
7 Tbsps.	sugar
2 Tbsps.	brown sugar
7 ozs.	cream
1½ Tbsps.	flour
⅞ cup	sliced almonds
⅞ cup	shredded coconut

Combine in a saucepan the butter, sugar, and one half the cream. Beat until creamy. Add the flour, and cook. Remove from heat, and add the rest of the cream, toasted almonds, and coconut. Spread over baked cake. Brown lightly under the broiler.

HIGBEE'S
IS 100 YEARS OLD TODAY

White Layer Whipped Cream Cake (serves 8-10)

2 cups	sifted cake flour
2 tsps.	baking powder
¼ tsp.	salt
1½ cups	sugar
½ cup	water
1 tsp.	vanilla
1 cup	whipping cream whipped stiff
3	egg whites (use large eggs)

Preheat oven to 350 degrees. Grease and flour two 8- or 9-inch round cake pans. Sift together first three dry ingredients. Sift again with the sugar. Set aside. Add vanilla to the water, and set aside. Whip egg whites stiff, and set aside. Whip the cream, and fold into the egg whites. Add the cream/egg white mixture to the dry ingredients alternately with the water/vanilla mixture, and mix and fold until well blended. Divide batter between the two baking pans. Bake at 350 degrees for 25-30 minutes or until lightly browned. Cool for 10 minutes, and remove from pans to wire racks to finish cooling. Use frosting of your choice or Cinnamon Apple Cream.

Cinnamon Apple Cream Topping and Filling

3	medium cooking apples
1 cup	water
1 cup	sugar
⅛ cup	red cinnamon drops (may substitute 8 round cinnamon disc hard candies)
1 cup	whipping cream

Combine water and sugar and candies, and put aside, stirring occasionally. Peel and core the apples, and cut into quarters. Cut each quarter into 4 sections. By this time, the candies should be dissolved. Cook the syrup until the sugar is dissolved and the mixture is bubbly. Carefully add the apple slices, and continue cooking. When the apple slices are tender and transparent, remove from syrup, and drain on a wire rack until cool. Reserve 8-10 of the more perfect pieces for use as a garnish, and chop the remainder. Whip the cream stiff, and add 1 cup of the chopped apples and sugar to taste. Mix lightly, and spread between the layers and on the top of the cake. Garnish with the slices. Chill for 2 hours.

Cakes and Frostings

CHILDREN'S PARTY LUNCHEON
85¢
SERVED ON SPECIAL LITTLE DISHES

First you set your table from the little sideboard,
then you eat:—

Creamed Chicken, Mashed Potatoes
Fresh Peas and Carrots

A Teeny Tiny Whole Loaf of Bread with Butter

A Pot of Cool Cocoa
and for Dessert,

An Ice Cream Cake
with Three Candles

One for You, One for Me,
and One for All the
Other Little Children
in the World

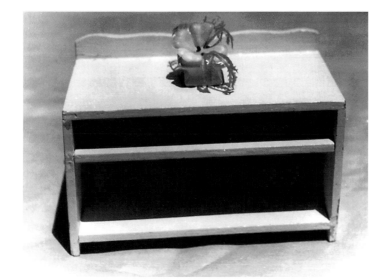

Pies

Banana Cream Pie

2½ cups	milk
½ cup	sugar
2	egg yolks
2 Tbsps.	cornstarch
1 tsp.	vanilla
1	medium size banana, mashed
1	baked/prepared pie shell

Combine sugar and cornstarch in a bowl. Pour into a pan. Mix together eggs and milk, and add to the dry ingredients. Mix together well. Cook over medium heat until thick and bubbly. Remove from heat, and add the vanilla. Cover with plastic wrap, and cool. Place the sliced bananas into the baked pie shell. Pour filling over the bananas, and chill. Garnish with whipped cream.

Note: The Silver Grille kitchen staff prepared pie crusts from a mix made weekly from shortening, pastry flour, and salt. We suggest you use your favorite pie crust recipe, pie crust mix, or already prepared pie shell.

Cappuccino Pie

Crust:

1¼ cups	chocolate wafers, crushed
⅓ cup	margarine

Icing:

1 cup	chocolate syrup
¼ cup	coffee liquor

Filling:

¼ cup	coffee liquor
1 oz.	whipped cream
1 quart	coffee ice cream

Pie Shell:

Crush cookies in a chopper. Mix softened margarine and crushed cookies. Pour mixture into a buttered 9-inch pie pan. Press mixture firmly with a spoon over the bottom and sides of the pie pan. Do not make a thick crust. Bake 8 minutes, and cool.

Filling:

Soften the 1 quart of coffee ice cream, and stir in the coffee liquor. Pour into the cooled crust and freeze. After the pie is frozen, combine the icing ingredients, and pour the icing mixture over the top, and freeze again. Cut the pie into eighths, and use a pastry bag to apply the whipped cream topping.

Cheese Dream Pie

1 Tbsp.	gelatin
¼ cup	cold water
1 lb.	creamed cottage cheese
2	egg yolks, beaten until thick and yellow colored
6 Tbsps.	sugar
⅓ cup	hot milk
⅓ cup	cold milk
2	egg whites, beaten stiff
6 Tbsps.	sugar
1 cup	whipping cream
1 tsp.	vanilla

Combine gelatin and cold water, and set aside. In a mixing bowl, whip the cottage cheese. In another pan, whip together the egg yolks and the first amount of sugar. Add the hot milk, and cook over hot water until the spoon is coated. Remove from stove,

add the gelatin mixture, and stir. Add the cold milk. Beat egg whites until stiff, and add the second amount of sugar. Beat the whipping cream stiff. Fold the whipping cream and egg whites into the egg yolks and cheese mixture all at the same time and pour into the graham cracker crust (see recipe following Dutch Apple Pie). Refrigerate.

Note: This will make a very full pie. If you have some extra filling, it can be poured into a serving dish and enjoyed separately.

Chocolate Chocolate Cream Pie

10 Tbsps.	sugar
5 Tbsps.	cocoa
3½ Tbsps.	cornstarch
⅛ tsp.	salt
1½ cups	milk
1¼ cups	half and half
1	baked 9″ pie shell

Mix sugar, cocoa, cornstarch and salt. Add enough of the milk to dissolve the ingredients. Scald the rest of the milk and cream, and add to the above mixture. Cook until the mixture thickens. Pour into the baked pie shell. Cool, and top with whipped cream.

Dutch Apple Pie

3 lbs.	pie apples *(tester used Granny Smith)*
½ cup	sugar
⅓ cup plus 1 Tbsp.	flour
1 tsp.	lemon juice
1 tsp.	salt

Peel, core, and slice the apples for pie. Add the rest of ingredients, and mix well. Place in pie pan lined with your favorite pie crust. Then pour over the following mixture:

1 cup	sugar
5 Tbsps.	flour
¾ tsp.	salt
¾ tsp.	cinnamon
1 cup	half and half

Place the top crust over, seal, and vent. Bake 25 minutes at 450 degrees. Turn down to 350 degrees, and bake for another 30- 40 minutes, until nicely browned. Cut when cool.

Graham Cracker Crust (makes 1 9-inch pie)

1½ cups	crushed graham crackers
½ cup	sugar
½ cup	melted butter

Combine ingredients, and mix. Then press mixture firmly into a 9-inch pie tin. Sprinkle lightly with cold water, and bake in a 300-degree oven for 8 minutes. Cool on a rack before filling.

Lemon Chiffon Pie

1 Tbsp.	gelatin
2 Tbsps.	cold water
2	egg yolks
4 Tbsp.	sugar
Dash	salt
4½ Tbsps.	lemon juice
1 tsp.	grated lemon rind
4½ Tbsps.	sugar
2	egg whites

Mix gelatin in cold water. Heat egg yolks and sugar, and add to dissolved gelatin mixture. Heat lemon juice. Add to gelatin mixture with salt and lemon rind. Cool. Cook over medium heat, whisking constantly until thick and bubbly. Remove from heat and cool. When cool, but still liquidy, beat egg whites in a separate bowl. When egg whites are stiff, add the second sugar and continue beating until well mixed and stiff. Egg whites will appear glossy. Fold a small amount of the egg whites into the lemon gelatin mixture to lighten it. Then fold in the remaining egg white mixture. Pour into an already baked or prepared 8- or 9-inch pie shell. Chill. Garnish with whipped cream.

Lime Chiffon Pie

3 ozs.	lime gelatin
¼ cup	lemon juice
Dash	salt
3	egg yolks
2½ Tbsp.	sugar
3	egg whites
½ cup	sugar
1	pie shell

Mix lime gelatin with boiling water. Warm egg yolks with sugar and salt. Beat egg whites with sugar until stiff. Add the egg yolks to the gelatin mixture. Add the lemon juice, then fold into beaten egg whites, and pour into the pie shell. Chill.

Melt Away Chocolate Pie (serves 8)

1	pie crust
2 cups	flaked coconut
6 Tbsps.	melted margarine

Lightly (or coat) butter an 8- or 9-inch pie tin. Combine the coconut and melted margarine. Mix thoroughly, and press mixture into pie pan around the bottom and sides of the pan. Bake in a 325-degree oven approximately 10 minutes just until the crust is lightly brown in color. Cool thoroughly.

Filling:

1 tsp.	instant coffee
2 Tbsps.	boiling water
8 ozs.	chocolate mint candy
5 cups	whipped topping

In a small saucepan, dissolve the coffee powder in water, and add chocolate candy. Stir the chocolate mixture over low heat until melted. Cool. Fold in the whipped topping, and pile into the coconut crust. Freeze several hours or overnight (it will not freeze solid). Cut pie into 8 servings. Garnish with a large dollop of whipped cream in the center of the pie; then grate some of the chocolate candy and sprinkle on top of the whipped cream.